A World of Words: Animals

Illustrations by
Molly Smith

Montgomery Reed Press®

ISBN: 978-0-578-81521-3
First Edition

www.montgomeryreedpress.com

Deutsch

Español

Français

English

Nihongo

Italiano

日本語

A World of Words: **Animals**

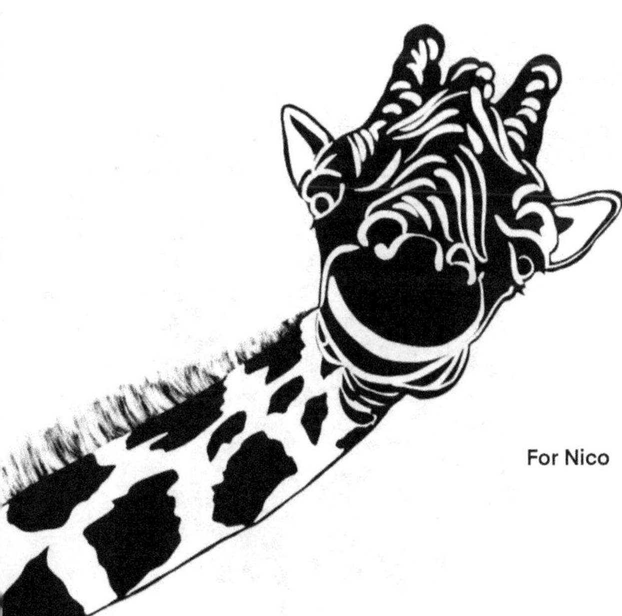

For Nico

das Kaninchen

el conejo

le lapin

the rabbit

il coniglio

usagi
ウサギ

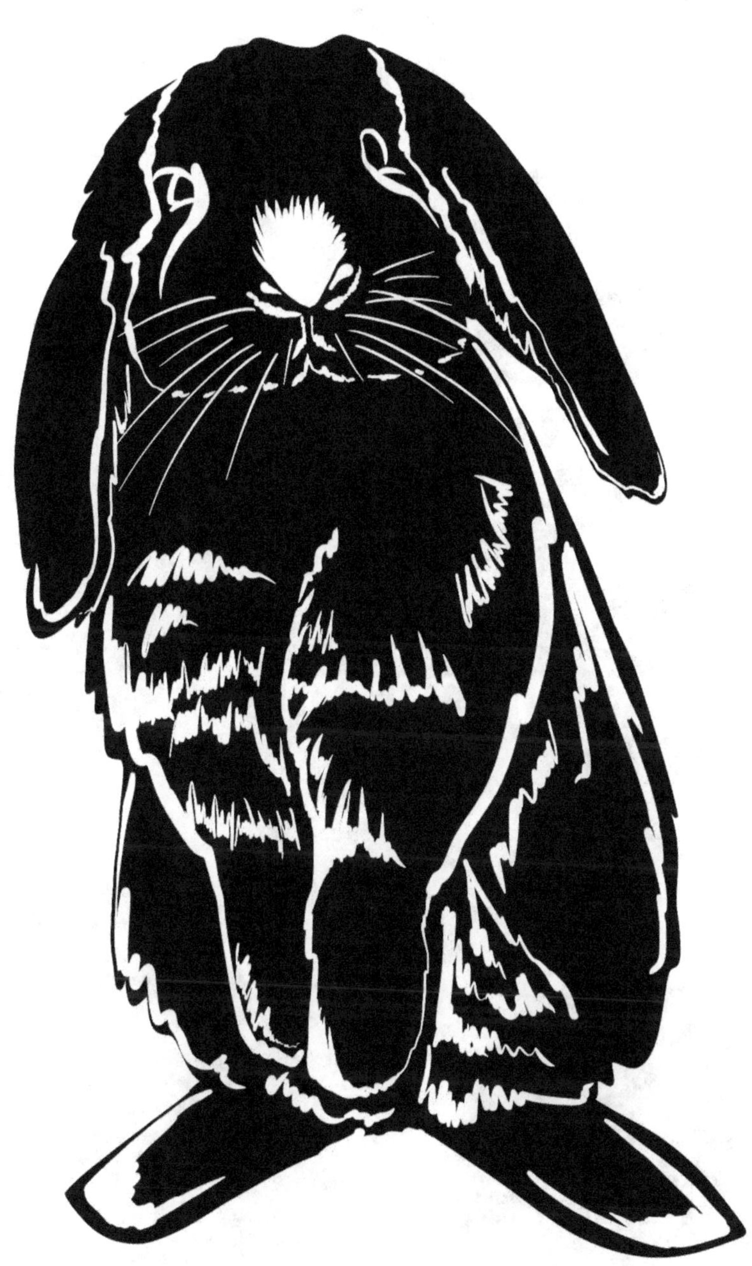

der Elefant

el elefante

l'éléphant

the elephant

l'elefante

zō

象

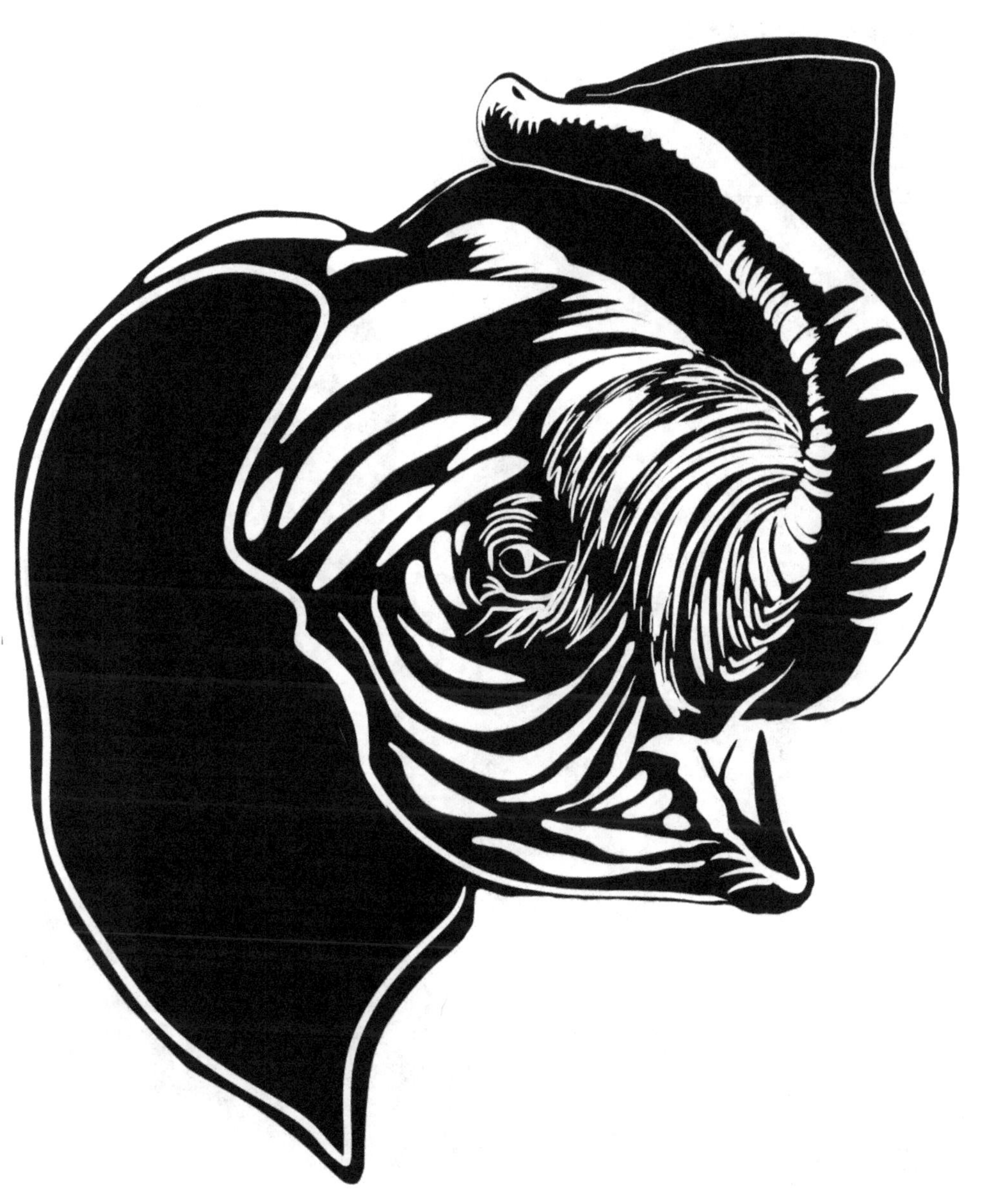

die Giraffe

la jirafa

la girafe

the giraffe

la giraffe

kirin

キリン

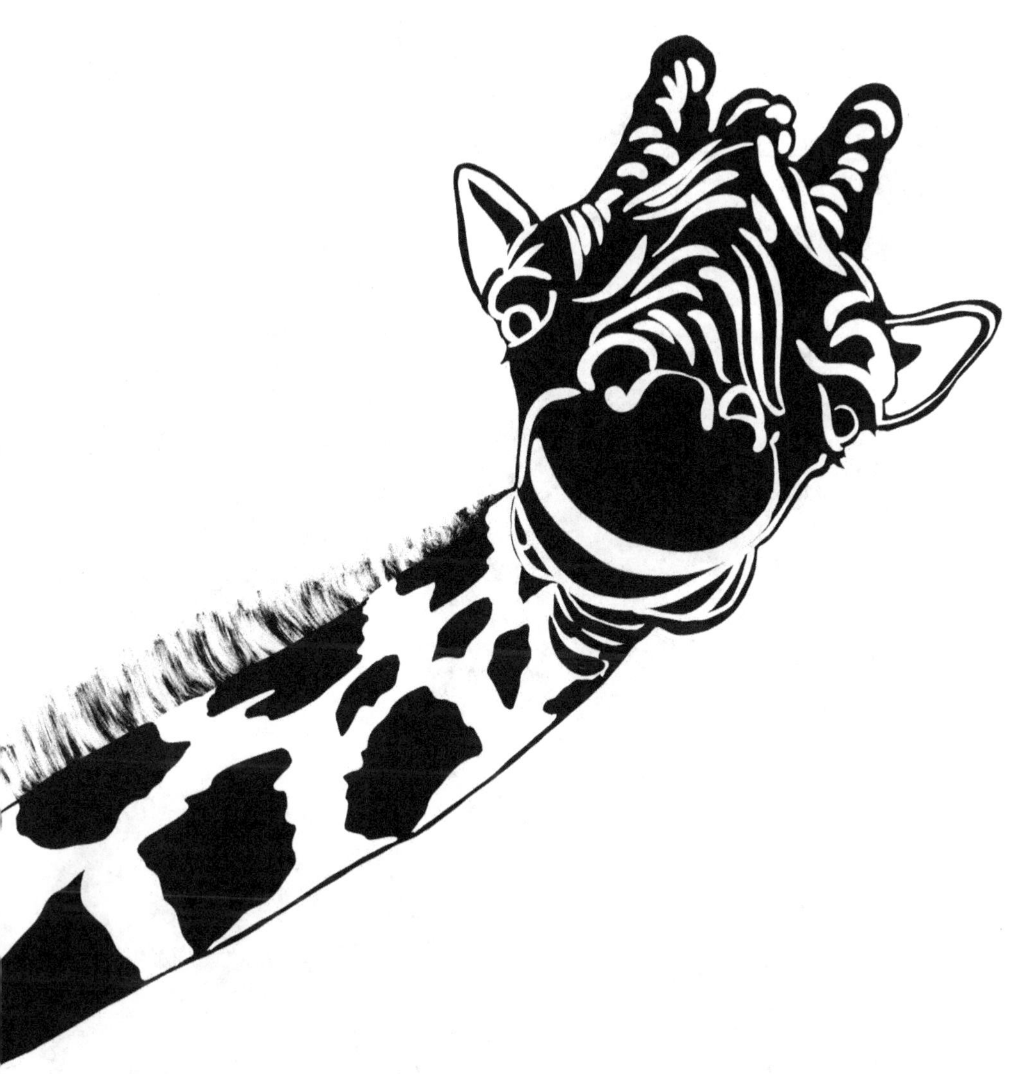

das Pferd

el caballo

le cheval

the horse

il cavallo

uma

うま

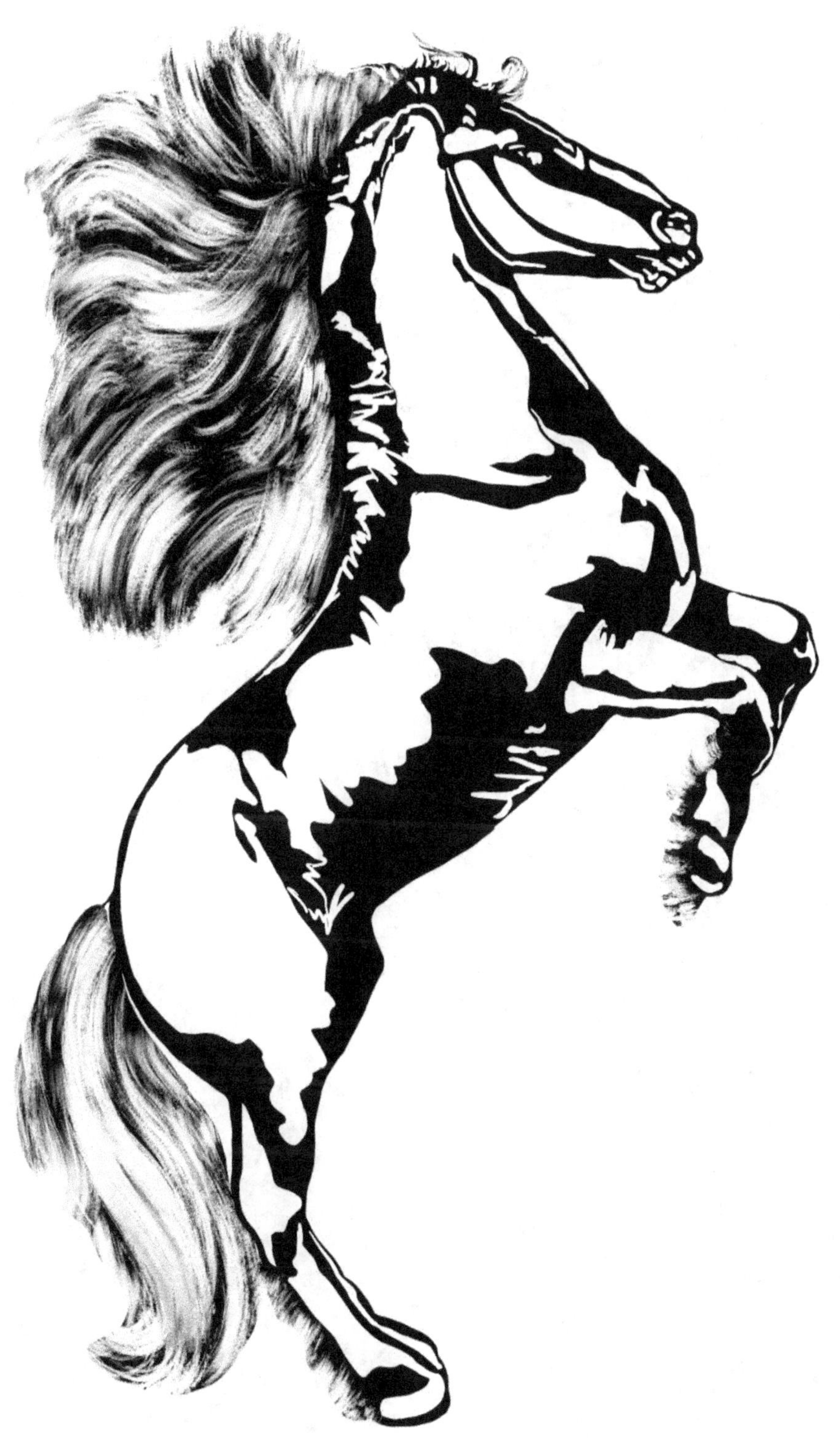

das Schwein

el cerdo

il cochon

the pig

il maiale

buta

豚

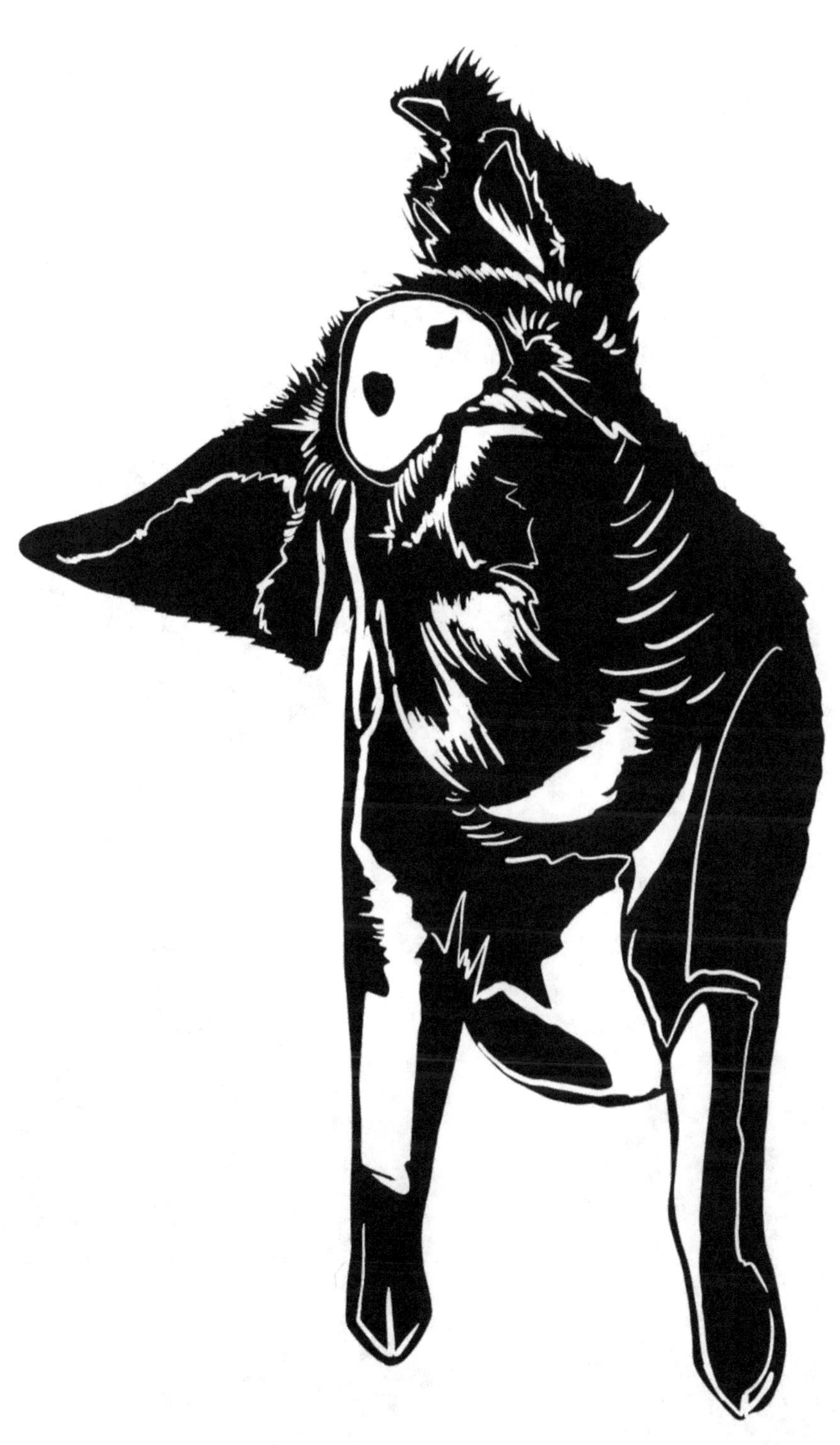

die Katze

el gato

le chat

the cat

il gatto

neko
ネコ

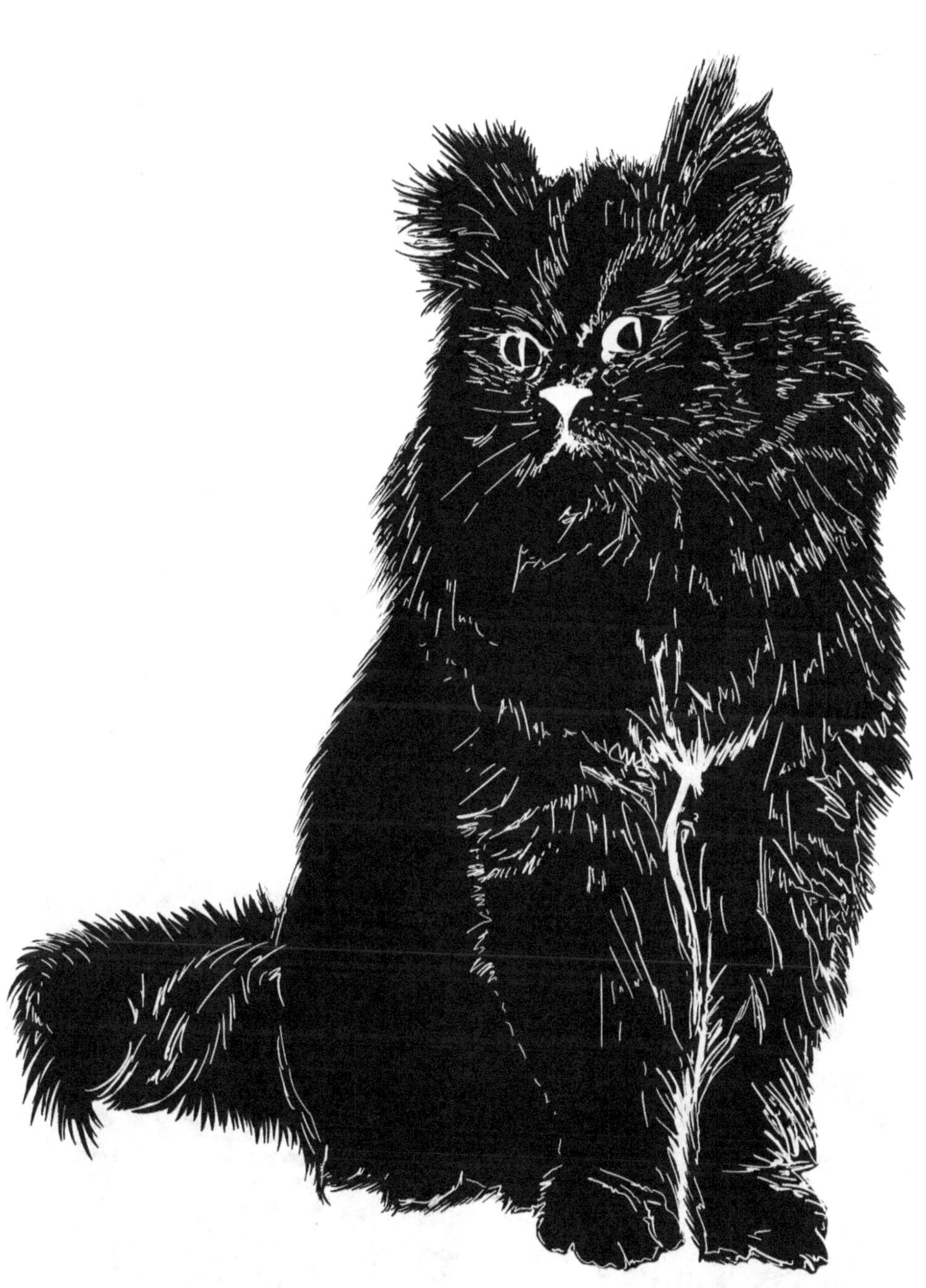

der Vogel

el pájaro

l'oiseau

the bird

l'uccello

tori

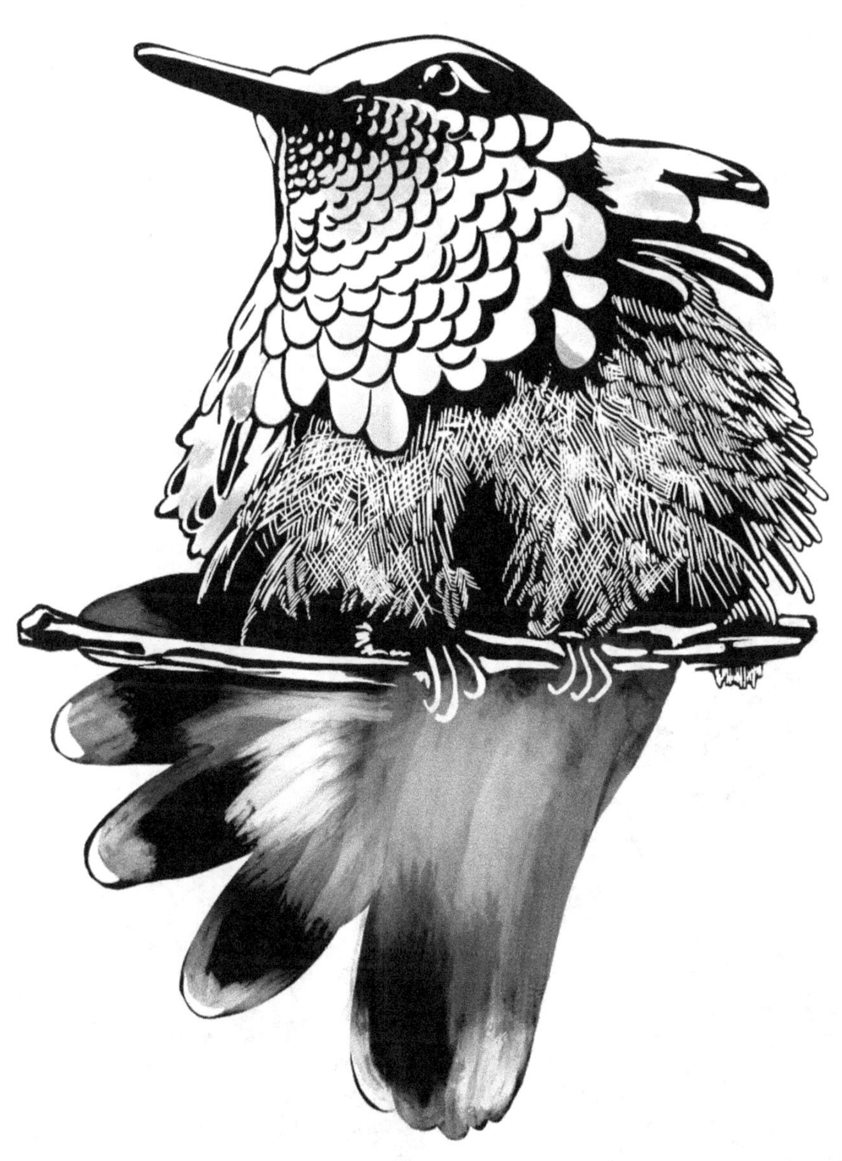

die Kuh

la vaca

la vache

the cow

ushi

牛

la mucca

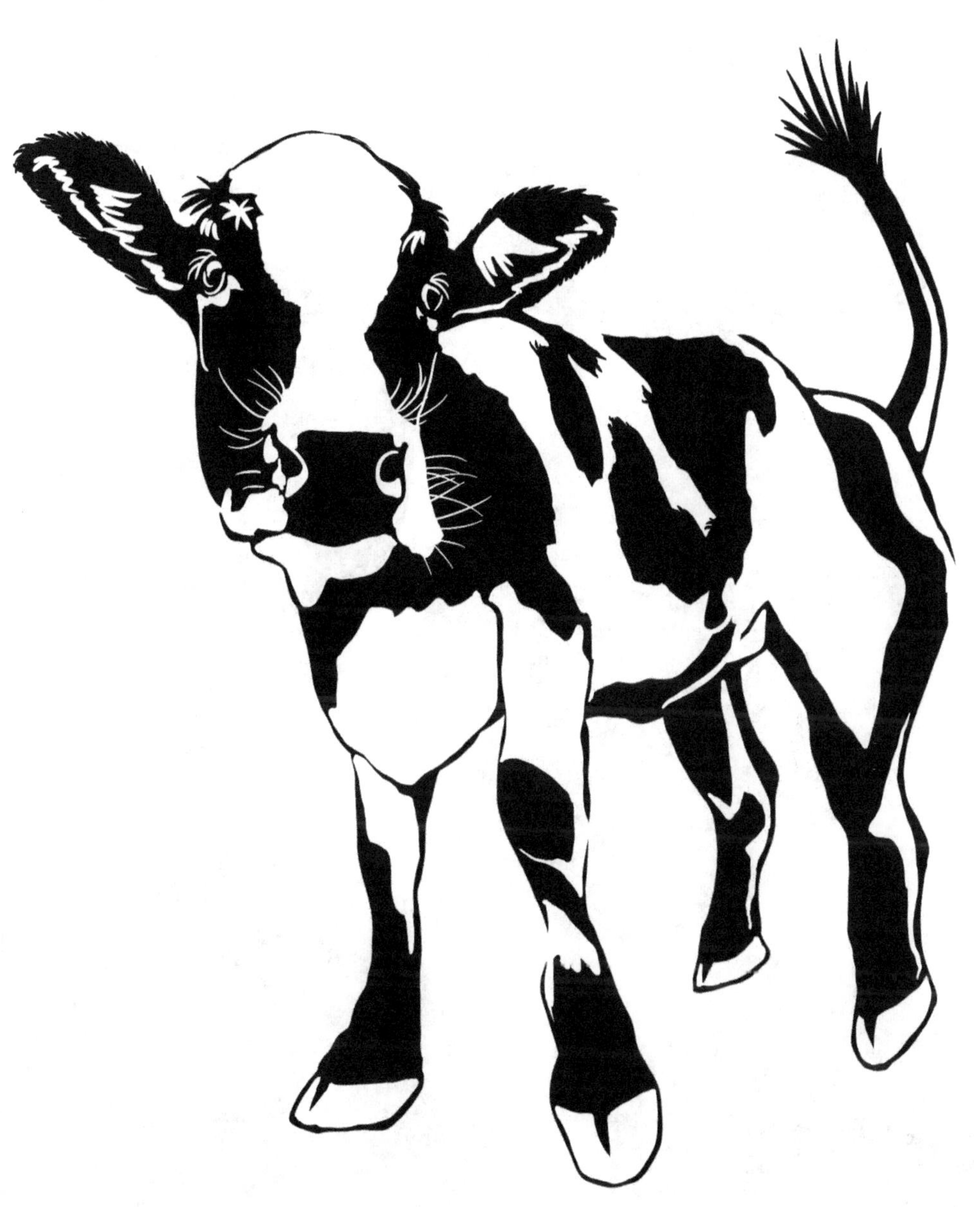

der Fisch

el pez

le poisson

the fish

sakana

魚

il pesce

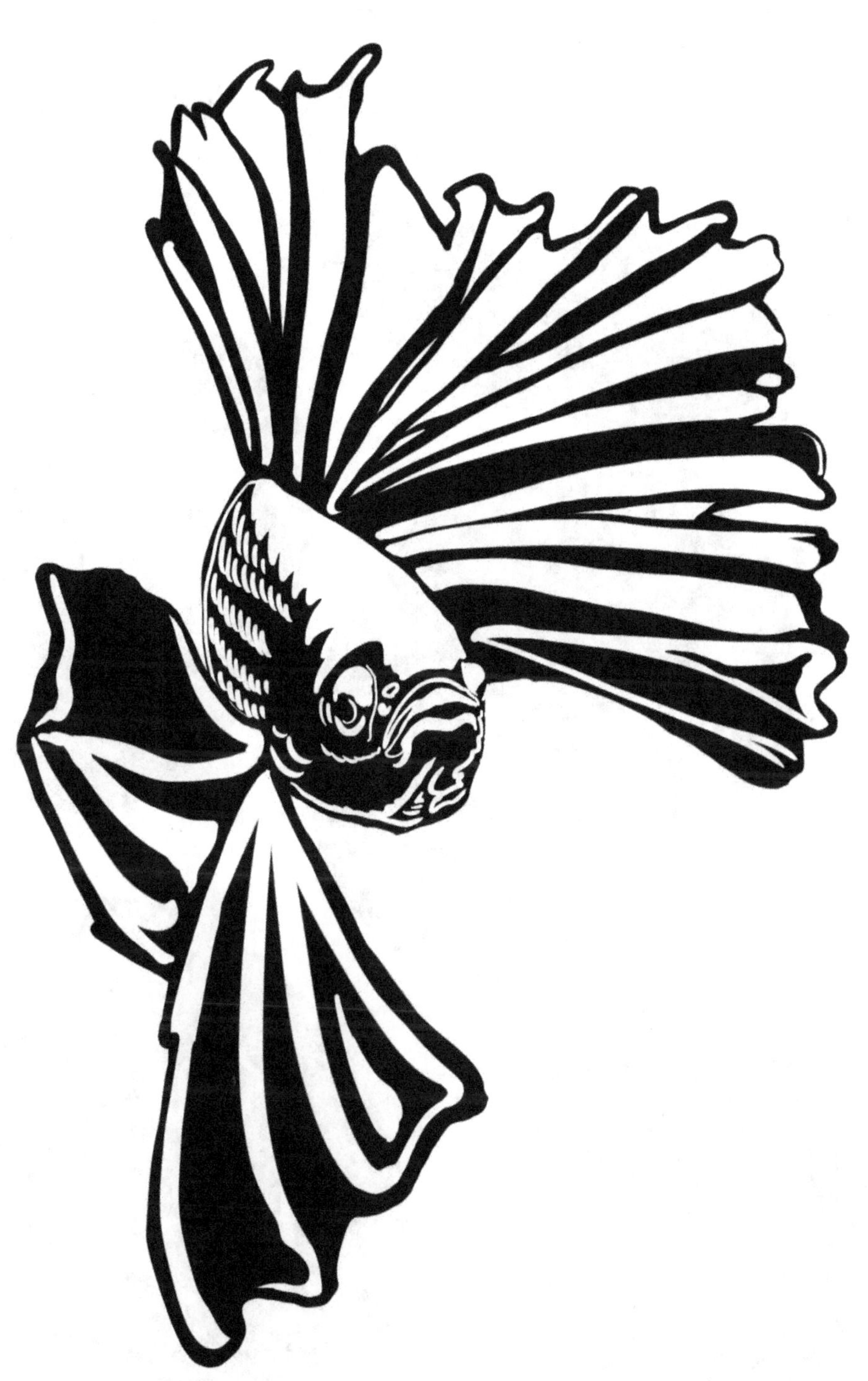

die Schildkröte

la tortuga

la tortue

the turtle

la tartaruga

kame
カメ

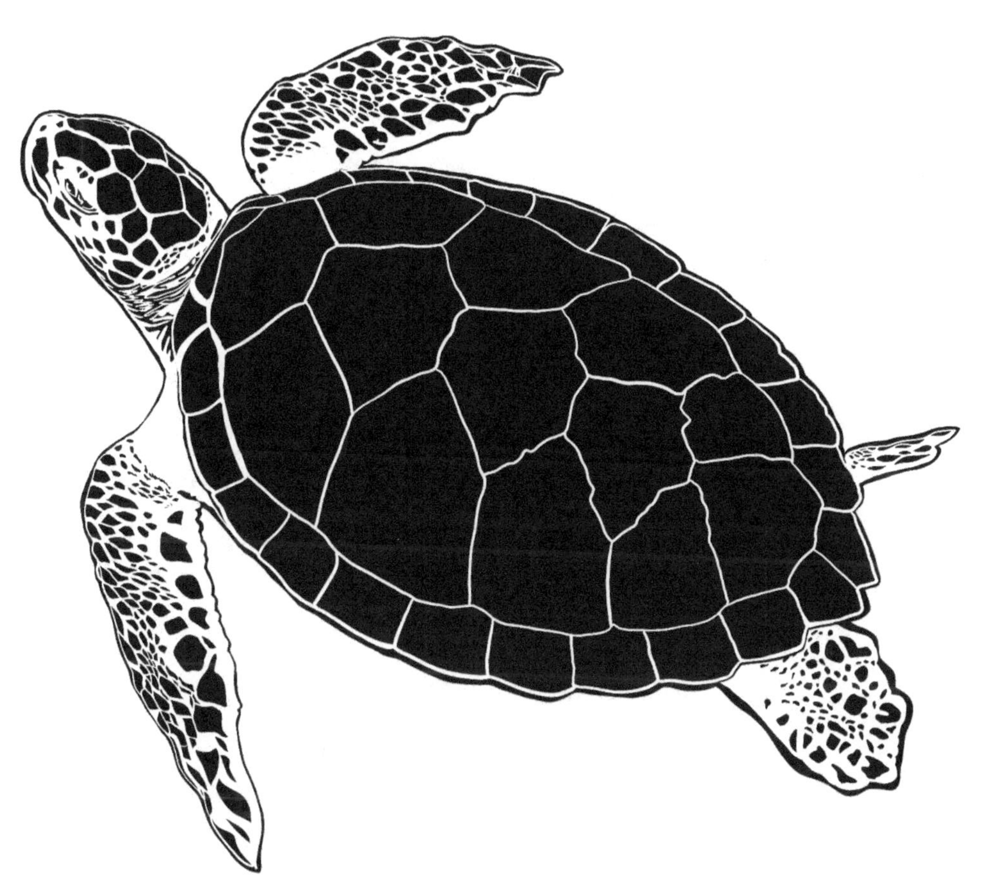

www.montgomeryreedpress.com

Coming soon

A World of Words:

Flowers
Transportation
Food
Insects

www.ingramcontent.com/pod-product-compliance
Lightning Source LLC
LaVergne TN
LVHW010550100826
845148LV00013B/2681